HOW TO DRIVE A MAN CRAZY IN BED

Easy tips to drive a man crazy, get a man horny, talk dirty, tease, please and make him always want you.

Jessica Tyler

COPYRIGHT

TABLE OF CONTENT

INTRODUCTION

Everything written in this book consists of everything I practiced myself personally and it worked for me. This is my personal experience over the years. That is why I have packed every one of the tips I know for you not to go through the stress of finding how to do it but getting it done immediately and as soon as possible. I am sure this will change your sex life.

Experience they say is the best teacher. This book is from my personal experience. So, you must believe me this will be a sure recommendation for you.

I got to understand that while driving a man crazy in bed, I am also being satisfied in the process. So it is not that he is the only one getting all the pleasure we both enjoy it together. Remember that the satisfaction of the two of you is necessary every time you both have sex. When only a person enjoys pleasure, then that is not sex, it is biased and it is not done the right way. Here is a self-help book that will give you the necessary guidelines.

I put all my expertise and experience into this book to help women have a lasting plus enjoyable relationship. This book depends on my own privileged insights on the best way to drive a man crazy in bed. I have used all stunts in this book and most likely glad to finish up as a winner most times.

I can say after my experience that driving a man crazy in bed gives your man fulfillment much beyond what you can envision. It will make a lady mindful of her capacity. It gives you the opportunity to do the things that you used to fantasize about.

This book will teach you also enjoy yourselves, how to tease him, please him, how to feel yourselves, how to turn him on as you turn yourself on also. It is a complete tip. Try it out.

CHAPTER 1
SPICE UP YOUR ROOM

Your bedroom should ideally be a place you can get a deeply connecting sexual intimacy and restful sleep. Take your time to arrange it always. Keep it neat and dress it all up.
MY WINNING TIPS:

1. Scents

Here's a cheat list for some pleasant scent.

Energizing scents: rosemary, orange, citrus, lemon.

Relaxing scents: vanilla, lavender, tea tree oil, jasmine, pumpkin.

2. Your massage oil should be handy

Sensual massage happens to be one of the best ways to relax your head and body while in the same way connecting with your man and engaging in foreplay.

Get your favorite oil or simply use coconut oil.

3. Get soft and quality sheets

Get a set of high thread, quality count sheets that your body enjoys when you lay on it or get in contact with it.

Please, avoid purchasing white sheets because, either you like it or not, white sheets will show stains. What will happen if your sex life is fun at all.

4. Romantic music

Sex and Music both get into the primal parts of our brain, that is why the two go so well together. Romantic music can add a whole lot of swagger to your bedroom.

Select whatever song makes you feel the sexiest.

It can be Melodic dubstep? Instrumental Spanish guitar music? Old school rock? Sexy R&B?

5. Keep your favorite sex toys close

It's fun to have some sex toys on hand to bring more adventure to your sex life

CHAPTER 2

DRIVE HIM CRAZY WITH YOUR DRESSING

There are different ways to be seductive in dressing. Each should make you feel full of confidence, poised, and comfortable.

Drawing attention to your best physical features by spicing up your wardrobe is a superb way to be seductive and sexy at the same time.

1. Strapless neckline

a classic strapless dress style helps to show off your kissable shoulders. These dresses bring attention to your sexy neck and collarbones and put you in the spotlight.

2. Cleavage reign

Never be afraid to get attention to your best features. Being confident in the way you appear is the epitome of being seductive.

Get a plunging V-neckline or side boob dress is best for women with shorter necks because outfits with the vertical drop add inches to the neck.

3. Show your legs

A sexy bodycon or mini bandage dresses are the best fix if your legs are your source of pride for your leg. They also show off your legs in a sexy way.

4. Seduce with rompers

Rompers, jumpsuits, or playsuits are also sexy if they look smart on you. They are casual but trendy and they also are perfect for showing off lots of legs.

5. Bare skin always works

A cut-out dress reveals your body seductively. It shows off delectable parts of skin thereby leaves plenty to the imagination.

6. A front zip dress

A perfect way to tickle the imagination is through seduction. Few other dresses do it just as a front zip bandage dress. Create sexy stirs with a zip running from a dress neckline to hem. It seduces perfectly!

7. Grab Seductive Lingerie

Putting on sexy underwear can boost your mood and make you look sexy. Lingerie has this awesome effect on almost everyone. Try this out and you will always not forget this tip.

CHAPTER 3
SURE TIPS TO MAKE HIM ALWAYS WANT YOU

The ability to get your man turned on in the bedroom is easy; just make sure you leave him always wanting you. Never let there be a second when he looks at you and doesn't ponder on being all over you.

Ensure you give him sexy compliments that give him flashbacks that you still notice him, and that the time you notice him, you want him to get down with you right there.

Follow these all-time working tips:

1. His masculinity:
This can be done in two ways, either strip away his manly power or enhance them more. Take them away by controlling him, tying him, and taking charge of sex. This can be done with blindfolds or other things to keep things interesting.

2. Build the eagerness and let him wait!
Eagerness and the steps to the actual sex most times frustrate men more than you know, but of course, this time, it's usually for a good course: the more they get frustrated, the wilder the sex will turn out to be.

An example of ways to build this anticipation is by sending him pictures that you don't send often but will surely leave him wanting more.

Text him and give a short description of what you will do to him as soon as he gets home. That will guarantee you will be on his mind all through.

3. Control the shower time:

The shower, which people feel doesn't matter sometimes could be the horny time you both need.

4. Let your fingers and hands work for you:

Heading to the penis is quite easy to turn a man on, but never forget about the other parts of his body. Trace the parts of his body. Trace your fingertips across his chest, hips, arms, and more. As you do that, you can move your hand closer to his penis, which will be pretty hard by then.

5. Scratch His Back Gently:

This might be strange to you, but many men are turned on when a woman scratches their back. Do this and pay attention to his response.

6. Talking dirty

Doing this is such a great move when you want to turn him on. More so, many men love it when their partners are courageous enough to talk dirty.

You can try out this example:
I wish to feel your cock inside me!
(This will turn your man on, while also firing up his ego at the same time).

CHAPTER 4

SEXIEST WAY TO TEASE HIM

Please, do not always tease your man. It can become frustrating if you always tease him. Perhaps he has a big project at hand or some family member came visiting for the summer. Ensure you tease him at a later time when he is in a better mood.

The important thing is to build up tension and release it. Surely, you'll feel pretty turned on after all the teasing!

If this is done correctly, this can lead to some romantic sessions in bed. As soon as he's able to grab you, the rest become sexy.

More tips:

If you are together at a bar or party, send him either a sex text that describes what you want him to do when you guys get home or, you can send a text like "beautiful shirt, it is pretty sure it'll look a lot better on the floor." This will make him want to have you down immediately.

Ask strange questions like "do you feel this countertop would be perfect place to get you down?

Men get easily aroused by visual stimuli. Play with him by bending pick up something on the floor in a very short skirt or. Behave like you don't know he's watching you and you'll be amazed how he'll be aroused.

When his friends come visiting, yell from your room that you need his assistance with something. The moment he enters, decorate him with a deep kiss and gently grab his package. Then make him return to his friends as nothing happened.

CHAPTER 5

MASTER HIS EROGENOUS / WEAK SPOTS

Lower Stomach

When you stimulate this area you make him feel super-pleasurable through kissing and gentle biting. You can even try out some light pressure play, "NOTE: it's advisable to try pressure play with an empty bladder to avoid pain"

Ears

There are sensitive skin outside the ear and numerous sensory receptors on the inside. For many people, the ears top the list of their erogenous zones.

Try lightly kissing or licking your man's earlobes and see how he will respond.

Foreskin

This consists of nerve endings that enhance pleasure for men with uncircumcised penises. The layer of skin gives the chance to mix it up for different sexual sensations during a blow job.

Scrotum and testicles

This part of a man's body is filled with highly-sensitive nerves that are always waiting to be enjoyed. During a blow job, gently massage them, or while masturbating.

The bottom line

Human bodies consist of several sexually charged parts waiting to be explored. Be practical by taking time to know which spots work for you and your partner, then proceed to a show-and-tell to make the most of them.

CHAPTER 6

THE POWER OF HOT MASSAGE

Face

Use one or two fingers from each hand, press gently into your man's penis for several seconds continuously. Now, trace your fingers down their cheeks slowly at the same time.

Front of their neck

This stimulates the thyroid when caressed, which is a tiny neck gland that regulates sex drive, including energy and body functions. Begin by gliding circles around his Adam's apple if they have one with a finger. Next, use your lips along the throat and massage the area with your tongue.

The ear

Gently pull the earlobe between your forefinger and thumb, in the same moment, use your tongue to glide the C-shaped area on the outer layer of his ear. NOTE: Might tickle at first, but go slower and lighter.

The stomach

Gently place two fingers from his abdomen to the base of your man's penis. Now, with your fingertips, as you move toward his outer abdomen, circle his belly button, ensure the circles become bigger and bigger. It's necessary to reduce speed and pressure here so as not to only tickle him. You want him to moan not laugh.

The knees

The skin behind the knees has sensitive nerve endings. Make your partner lie on his chest, then slowly scratch behind his knee one at a time to produce some heat there before gently using your tongue back and forth in small circles across the area.

Soles of his feet

There is a line from the feet to other erogenous parts of the body. Glide your knuckles from your man's heel to the pad of his foot underneath his toes. Rub the pad in circles with your thumbs.

To avoid tickling him, use strong pressure. For an extra erotic scene, draw his big toe toward you, and plant some soft licks or a soft kiss.

CHAPTER 7

TALKING DIRTY AND SEXY

The words you say to your partner when in a romantic mood are not just words but sparks that turn their charge on. Men read meaning to those words and u can pull his sex trigger with words.

Now here are some nasty, dirty things to say to him:

On Bed:
1. I need your cock right now!
2. I want you to make me cum baby.
3. Will you fuck me hard?
4. I'm in love with your cock.
5. Cum all over my face.
6. I'm so wet.
7. I want to taste your cock.
8. Hold my hair and fuck me hard. (if you love rough sex).
9. Can we spend the weekend together completely naked!

Dirty Talk When not home together:

1. Can we go home already? I feel like doing some terrible things to you.
2. I feel like ripping your clothes off this minute.
3. If we were home, I'd have your cock in my mouth now.
4. Going out today is not a good idea; all I need now is your cock.
5. If you continue looking at me that way, we will need to go somewhere private.
6. Whisper: Do you know I'm not wearing panties?

CHAPTER 8

BLOW JOB HE WON'T FORGET

Most men enjoy blow jobs because it feels like sex, but it is a different experience. Giving your partner a blowjob is a great sexual gift you can offer him.

The wonderful thing about focusing majorly on giving oral to the head of your partner's penis is that you need not worry about taking it fully into your throat or mouth, so you need not worry much about choking or coughing.

Below are the best tips on how to give the best blow job your man will ever have (I swear)—and making it more enjoyable for yourself in the act:

1. Display interest in giving him a blow job

The number one rule for giving a good head is to behave like you surely want to do it.

The biggest complaint I heard from male clients concerning blow jobs has nothing to do with the way it is done, not skill has to do with their partner's interest in it. Men will have a wonderful time if they are aware their partner is enjoying it.

Make eye contact, tell him how turned on you are, and ask him what he wants.

2. Penis tip

The upper part of a man's penis is undeniably the most sensitive and we know more sensitivity directly means more pleasure. Use your tongue and lips to do the work here.

3. Your hands

Truly it is called oral sex but that doesn't mean your mouth must do all the work. The hands give you a tight grip and mouth gives wetness.

Once you've warmed up a bit, here's your basic stroke:

1.   With your dominant hand, wrap it around his shaft, now add your mouth.

2.   Connect your lips to your hand—that is, press your thumb-index finger (making an O sign) against your lips and keep them closed there.

3.   Slowly move your hand-and-lips up and down the penis.

4. Add spit (lots of it).

I could remember one of the first blow jobs I ever had (to a lady I'd been dating for seven months, so we were very comfortable with each other), I told her to spit on me. It freaked her out for a second—she wondered if spitting was a somewhat weird fetish—but then realized I just preferred it extra wet.

CHAPTER 9

LET THE SEX GAME BEGIN

Starting sex can be an awkward feeling. It does not count if you have been with your partner for long, starting can be a vulnerable thing and you are not alone here. The major factor is because we live in a world where men are often the initiators, which in turn makes them confident.

Initiating sex yourself removes pressure off your man, and it can mean the start-up of your routine. You can even control the way it goes, which can be very enjoyable and pleasurable!

If your partner is often the sex initiator, your partner will probably be happy when you are the new CEO (smiles). This might make things become somewhat more balanced between you two.

When You're Nervous About Initiating Sex

Being nervous before sex is normal, but you should not worry about starting sex, especially if it is a long-term partner. Reasons you might be nervous:

You don't want to be rejected: Of course, your partner might not want sex. He's human, and not every time humans want sex. On the other hand, feeling sick or tired can lead to rejection.

Scared of looking silly or foolish: Asking for sex can feel a little weird in some cases, but believe me, it's a skill you need to learn. You don't need to do it in person always. Call him, write a note or send a text message and this can help you save face until the day you're brave enough to start sex face-to-face.

How To Initiate Sex

There's no one specific way to get sex goin'. We've provided a few ideas, or you can come up with one on your own.

1. Be Direct

This route is often the best because sometimes guys can be a little oblivious to your hints. This can be realized if you've hinted at wanting sex earlier and he didn't pick up on it.

2. Use Body Language

When you're cuddling your man, amplify things up like going for his zipper, or grinding your hips against his penis. Grab his hands and place them on some part of your body – your breasts or vagina – that sends a clear message.

3. Press Yourself Against Him

Sometimes you feel your guy's boner against you when you are cuddling? His body wants sex. Take advantage of this too! Press your booty against his erected penis and put his hands on your breasts, the rest will become history.

4. Foreplay

Guys love stimulation. So unzip his pants and go down on him it's likely to be the beginning of some hot sex.

CHAPTER 10

SEX POSITIONS YOU SHOULD ALWAYS TRY

These are not just sex positions but they are positions that will set the bedroom on romantic fire.

Wheelbarrow

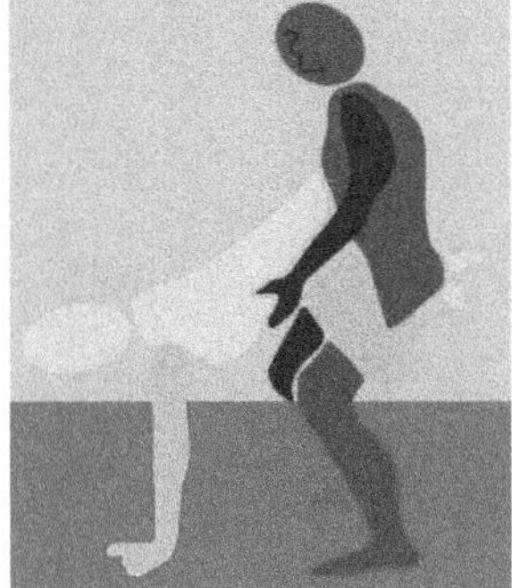

CAUTION: Never try this after an arm workout; your triceps will be weak

Doggy

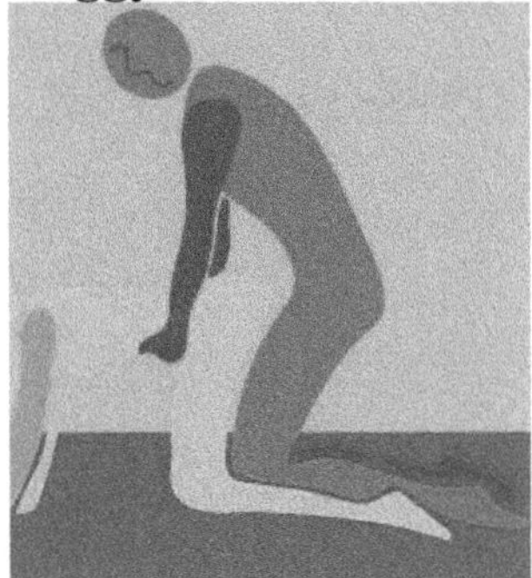

This style is a classic - your partner does all the work. It is one of the best-known positions for hitting the G-spot.

Cowboy

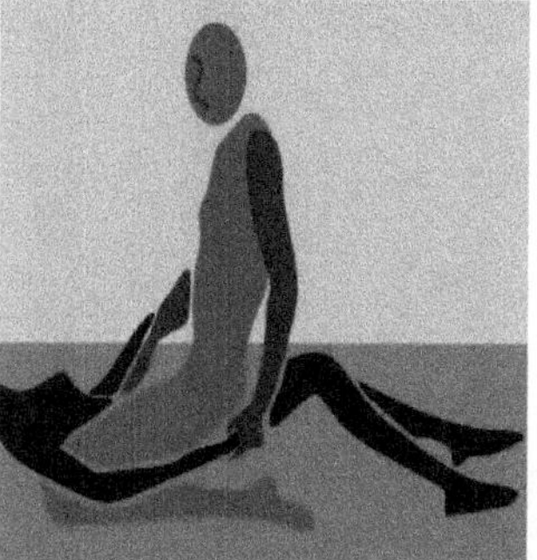

It is a known fact that one person is more satisfied than the other person i.e. the party under, but this position gives equal pleasure.

Leap Frog

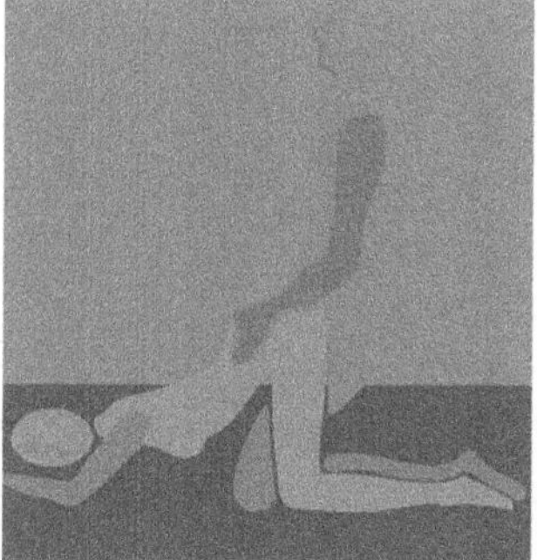

Here is a great position you will enjoy. You get to rest your head and arms on your pillow while your man does all the work.

Spread Eagle

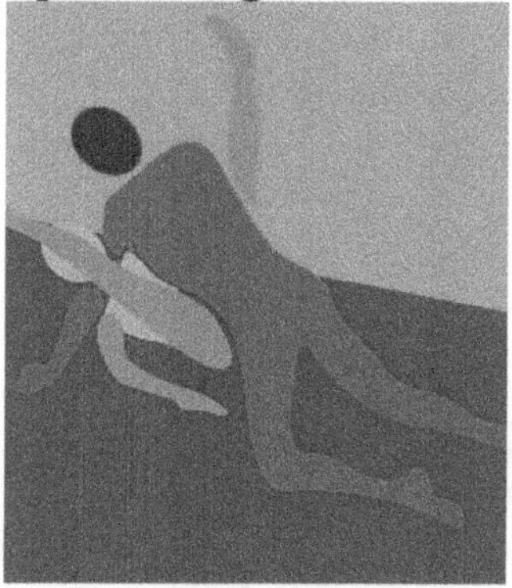

With this, you can skip your usual yoga flow as you are sure to get all the exercise you require and some deep thrust.

The Pretzel

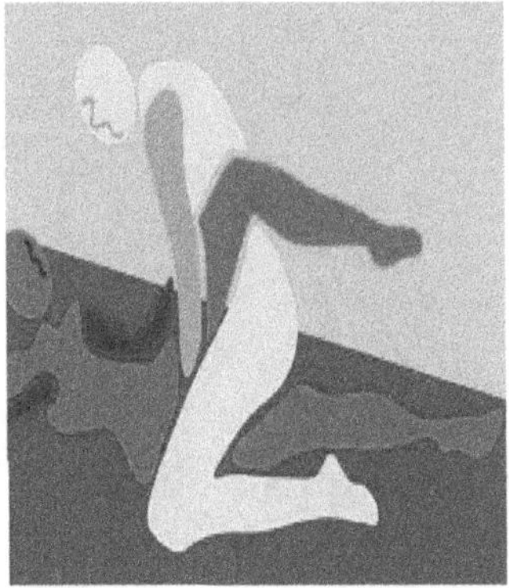

All required of you here is lie while your man does all the work.

Reverse Cowgirl

In a good way of course. Not everyone shows the most attractive facial expressions all through the process of sex, here is a perfect position to just not to worry about that.

CHAPTER 11
EYES SEDUCTION

Many ladies do not know turning on a man is much easier than a woman. All you need is to use the right words that will make them excited. Once you know this skill, getting him will get easier.

Ever working tips:
For a few seconds, hold your gaze, and don't be shy to look away from time to time. I do not mean you should stare but be sure he is aware you are looking at him and will continue looking for all the positive reasons.

When it comes to seduction, the eyes can be a useful tool. There are different ways your eyes can be used to display attraction and get your man to want you.

Initiate eye contact. Do not be shy. This shows confidence, which many men find attractive.
In addition to that, watching him from the corner of your eyes is helpful. Watch him from the corner of your eyes for some seconds.

My personal experience:
Give him a surprise at the door: "I could remember a day, as I got back from work, my girlfriend greeted me in lingerie and a sexy hairstyle. It passed a message to me that she wanted me and couldn't wait.

Bedroom striptease: "My partner stripped for me some time back and I really loved it!"

Sexy love note: "My girlfriend once wrote a note that said: "I appreciate you for introducing me to the pleasure in having my toes sucked.' This triggered my memory when we were together."

CHAPTER 12
EXTRA IRRESISTIBLE TIPS

Compliment them:
Directing pleasant sentiments toward individuals is misjudged. On the off chance that you like their butt, let them know! If their legs could on for quite a long time, tell them!

Enjoy hang out:
Because you're naked doesn't mean you HAVE to do something besides appreciate each other's conversation. Request takeout and stare at the TV, delighting in your completely naked selves.

Simply ask:
Why bother when you can just know?

Let him climb you:
You can make it far and away superior by drawing your knees toward your chest and getting a handle on the rear of your thighs. You can likewise put the bottoms of your feet on their chest in case you're in the mind-set for some profound entrance.

Silent treatment:
This is fundamentally sex pretenses: Wrap your hand around their penis and don't let out the slightest peep. At the point when they accomplish something you're truly into, give them a little press until you graduate to all-out handwork.

Cook together:
A holding action that is delightful. Likewise, an incredible reason to come up behind one another as you alternate creation that sandwich. Indeed, it very well maybe two hours before you eat, yet who's checking??

CHAPTER 13

HOW TO MAKE SEX FEEL GREAT FOR HIM

1. Change positions
In certain positions, you'll feel tighter, which will be decent for him. In some, he'll have the option to go further. In some, he'll have the option to feel different pieces of you all the more effectively (which he may truly like).

On the off chance that, for your pleasure, you should be in one situation to peak, that is alright! Simply start in an alternate position, and afterward switch later.

2. Squeeze his testicles (carefully!)
Discussing squeezing, in specific positions (like when you're on top) and your hands are free and more ready to arrive at things, give putting delicate weight a shot his balls. You must be cautious with this one, and it relies upon your man, however, numerous folks appreciate this.

3. Whisper in his ear
To make sex magnificent, attempt to use whatever number of faculties as could reasonably be expected. Utilize hearing! A murmur in his ear (murmuring is truly provocative). Indeed, even mention to him in detail what you're appreciating that he's doing.

4. Allow seeing your face when you reach climax
At last, here's the most extraordinary. It's not serious genuinely. It's seriously close to home, and that causes us to feel a lot nearer inwardly, which converts into more extraordinary creation love meetings. Let him observe your face when you peak.

CONCLUSION

After all these write-ups, I am sure your sex life won't remain the same and your man will be blown away by your new techniques. Be sure to recommend this book if truly you enjoy it.

Please leave a review on the website.

CONTACT:

For other enquiries:

Email: alwaysready153gmail.com

Thanks

www.ingramcontent.com/pod-product-compliance
Lightning Source LLC
Chambersburg PA
CBHW051942150726
47999CB00006B/2332